Impressionist Cats

after EDGAR DEGAS *Absinthe* 1876

Previous page: after PIERRE-AUGUSTE RENOIR *The Parisian Girl* 1874

Impressionist Cats

SUSAN HERBERT

A Bulfinch Press Book
Little, Brown and Company
Boston · Toronto · London

Preface

The love of the French for their pets is well known, so it is not surprising to find cats present in all the familiar scenes and subjects of the Impressionist painters. It takes no more than the slightest stretch of the imagination to suppose that Renoir, upon seeing a cat intrude mischievously upon his boating party scene, said to himself, "Of course! So much more charming with cats." Or we may think of Monet, perhaps accompanied by his own cats on a stroll in the country, realizing how his pets wander among the wild poppies with more pleasure and style than the people he has just painted. "Once more with cats!" he must have decided.

It was the late Professor Harvey Fishbone, himself an eminent art historian at the turn of the century, who first realized just how extensive the Impressionist cat *oeuvre* really was. There was hardly a great painter of the period who did not at some point surrender to the urge to populate Impressionism with cats, and yet these pictures were unappreciated and unsold. Fortunately for us, Professor Fishbone had sufficient means to travel extensively in France beginning in 1895 and at that time he started to assemble what was to become a unique and magnificent collection of Impressionist cat paintings, the gems of which are published in this book.

The Fishbone Museum, specially built to house the collection, has remained an intriguing mystery for many years, since the Professor decided that only cats should be permitted to view the paintings. Once a month, while their owners waited patiently outside, a lucky group of cats prowled through the exhibition rooms and purred with delight and recognition.

Now there has been a welcome change of heart and the Museum is planning to publish a catalogue raisonné of the entire collection, a massive scholarly work intended for students, experts, and serious art lovers, which will take me and my staff many years to accomplish. But it has been decided in the meantime to issue this selection of works, both as a tribute to the beloved founder of the Museum and to satisfy the great curiosity which the collection has aroused for such a long time.

Professor Hippolyte Féline
(Curator of the Fishbone Museum)

after MARY CASSATT *The Loge* c.1882

after
MARY CASSATT
The Bath
*c.*1891

after
PAUL CÉZANNE
The Card Players
1890-5

after
PAUL CÉZANNE
Woman with a Coffee Pot
1890-5

after
Edgar Degas
The Orchestra of the Paris Opéra
*c.*1869

after
EDGAR DEGAS
The Millinery Shop
*c.*1882

after
PAUL GAUGUIN
Tahitian Women
1891

after
VINCENT VAN GOGH
Self-portrait
1889

after
Vincent van Gogh
The Threshold of Eternity
1890
(after the drawing *Old Man with
his head in his Hands* 1882)

after
EDOUARD MANET
Nana
1877

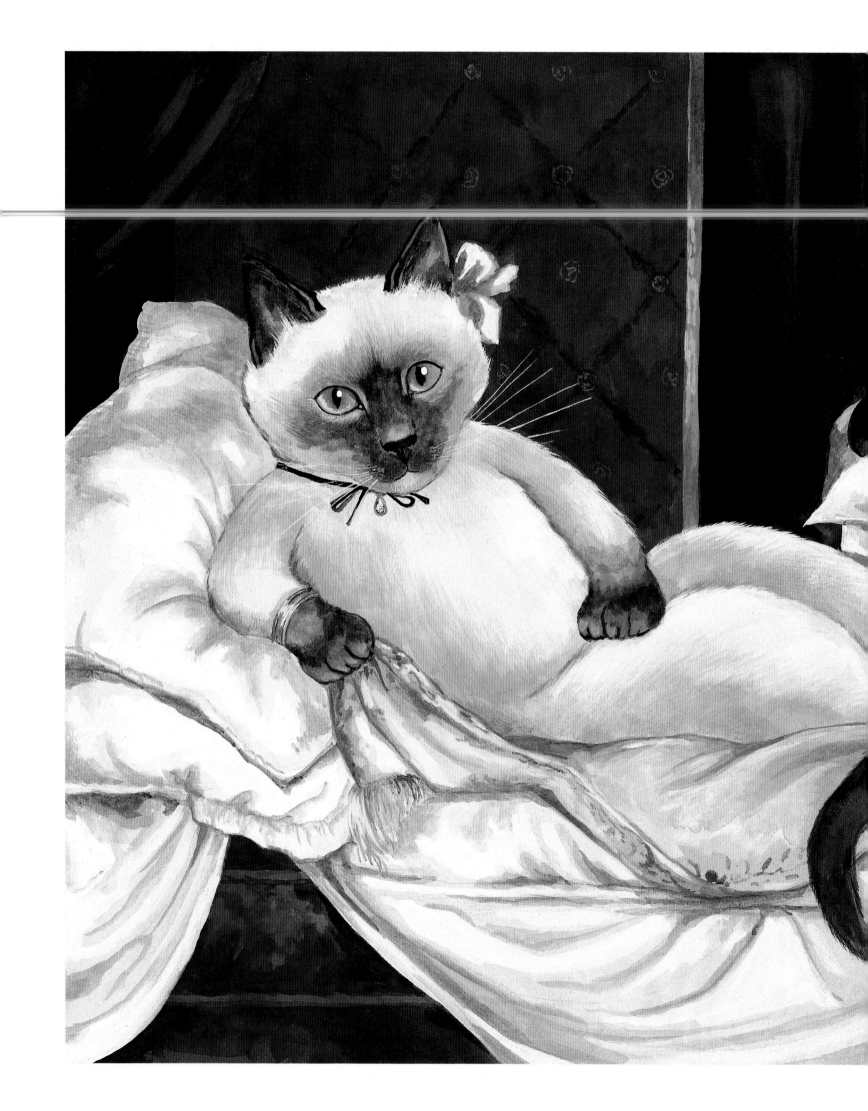

after
EDOUARD MANET
Olympia
1863

after
EDOUARD MANET
Lola de Valence
1861-2

after
EDOUARD MANET
The Fifer
1866

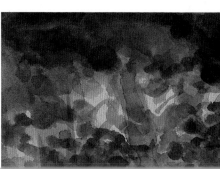

after
EDOUARD MANET
Luncheon on the Grass
1863

after
EDOUARD MANET
Eva Gonzalès
1869-70

after
CLAUDE MONET
Woman in a Green Dress
1866

after
CLAUDE MONET
The Promenade
(Madame Monet and her Son)
1875

after
CLAUDE MONET
Woman in a Garden, Springtime
*c.*1875

Susan Herbert

after
CLAUDE MONET
Wild Poppies
1873

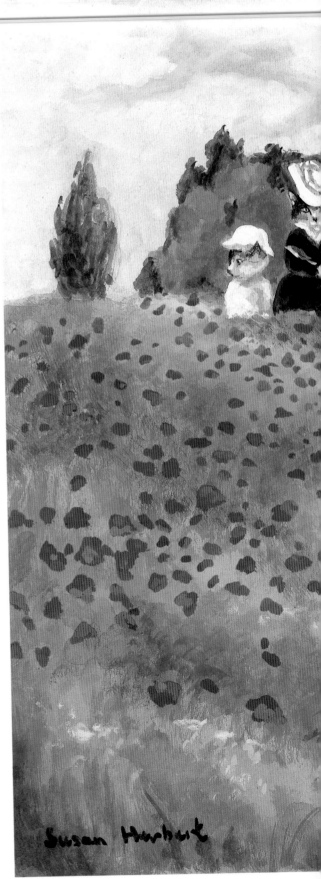

Susan Herbert

after
BERTHE MORISOT
The Cradle
1872

after
CAMILLE PISSARRO
Girl with a Stick
1881

after
PIERRE-AUGUSTE RENOIR
The Engaged Couple
(The Sisley Family)
*c.*1868

Susan Herbert

after
PIERRE-AUGUSTE RENOIR
Dancing at Bougival
1883

after
PIERRE-AUGUSTE RENOIR
The Lovers
*c.*1875

after
PIERRE-AUGUSTE RENOIR
Girls at the Piano
1892

after
PIERRE-AUGUSTE RENOIR
The Umbrellas
1879

after
PIERRE-AUGUSTE RENOIR
Madame Charpentier and Her Children
1878

after
PIERRE-AUGUSTE RENOIR
The Boating Party
1880-1

after
HENRI DE TOULOUSE-LAUTREC
At the Bar
1898

after
HENRI DE TOULOUSE-LAUTREC
In the Salon at the Rue des Moulins
1894

First North American Edition

ISBN 0-8212-1958-8

Library of Congress Catalog Card Number 92-53069
Library of Congress Cataloging-in-Publication information is available.

Bulfinch Press is an imprint and trademark of
Little, Brown and Company (Inc.)

Published simultaneously in Canada by
Little, Brown & Company (Canada) Limited

PRINTED IN HONG KONG